MEAN MACHINES

BOATS

MARK MORRIS

www.raintreepublishers.co.uk
Visit our website to find out more information about **Raintree** books.

To order:
 Phone 44 (0) 1865 888113
 Send a fax to 44 (0) 1865 314091
 Visit the Raintree Bookshop at **raintreepublishers.co.uk** to browse our catalogue and order online.

First published in Great Britain by Raintree,
Halley Court, Jordan Hill, Oxford OX2 8EJ,
part of Harcourt Education.
Raintree is a registered trademark of
Harcourt Education Ltd.

© Harcourt Education Ltd 2004
The moral right of the proprietor has been asserted.

Editorial: Charlotte Guillain and Richard Woodham
Design: Michelle Lisseter and Bridge Creative Services Ltd
Picture Research: Bea Ray and Pete Morris
Production: Jonathan Smith
Index: Indexing Specialists (UK) Ltd

Originated by Ambassador
Printed and bound in Hong Kong, China by
South China Printing Company

ISBN 1 844 43164 9
08 07 06 05 04
10 9 8 7 6 5 4 3 2 1

British Library Cataloguing in Publication Data
Morris, Mark
Boats – (Mean Machines)
I. Title
623.8'2

A full catalogue record for this book is available from
the British Library.

Acknowledgements
Aker Finnyards p. 41 (top); Art Directors and Trip pp. 32, 40; Boeing pp. 16–17, 50, 50–51, 51; Corbis pp. 4–5 (Neil Rabinowitz), 5 (middle) (Patrick Ward), 6 (Ludovic Maisant), 7 (Yogi.Inc), 10 (bot) (Bettman), 12 (top) (Hulton Getty), 13, 17, 20 (top), 24, 27, 28 (Yogi.Inc), 30–31 (Patrick Ward), 31, 41 (Chris Rainier), 42 (Bettman), 43 (Sygma), 44 (top) (Lowell Georgia), 44 (bot) (Neil Rabinowitz), 49, 54, 54–55 (Najlay Feanny), 55, 57(Amos Nachaum); Fastship p.57; Hovercraft International p. 34; Hulton-Getty pp. 5 (bot), 10 (top), 16, 25, 28–29, 34, 48; Kockums p. 23; Lockheed-Martin pp. 5 (top), 22; Maritime Museum pp. 8, 8 (top), 11; Mary Evans Picture Library pp. 14, 14–15; PA Photos pp. 12, 15, 32, 33, 35, 45, 47, 48–49; PPL pp. 36, 37, 38, 46; Rex Features pp. 39, 42; Science Photo Library pp. 25 (top), 26, 30; SOVFOTO pp. 52–53, 53; Sylvia Cordaiy Picture Library 108969 p. 37; United States Navy pp. 6, 18, 18 (top), 20, 21; VRI p. 38 (top).

Cover photograph of a speedboat reproduced with permission of Digital Vision/Robert Harding.

Every effort has been made to contact copyright holders of any material reproduced in this book. Any omissions will be rectified in subsequent printings if notice is given to the publisher.

Disclaimer
All the Internet addresses (URLs) given in this book were valid at the time of going to press. However, due to the dynamic nature of the Internet, some addresses may have changed, or sites may have changed or ceased to exist since publication. While the author and publisher regret any inconvenience this may cause readers, no responsibility for any such changes can be accepted by either the author or the publisher.

CONTENTS

Any words appearing in the text in bold,
like this, are explained in the Glossary.
You can also look out for them in the Up To
Speed box at the bottom of each page.

THE WORLD OF BOATS

SEE FOR YOURSELF

Many famous ships are still thrilling passengers, long after their travelling days are over. They are turned into floating museums and the public can go on board and tour them.

Welcome to the amazing world of brilliant boats. The best boats do not just go fast, they go the fastest. They do not just dive under water, they dive the deepest. They have more sails, more engines, more power. They are the biggest, the heaviest, the most expensive or the very first to achieve something.

Boats come in many different shapes and sizes. The only thing they have in common is the water.

- Some dive underneath it.
- Some cut straight through it.
- Some skim across the surface.

But they all make the best use of it.

WHERE ARE THEY?

So where should you go to see boats? Good sense tells us that water is the best place. So keep your eyes open near the **coast**. Have a closer look at the ships in ports and harbours. Or see if there a large lake near to you, with a sailing club.

Another excellent place to see amazing boats is at a museum. In fact, many boats are museums themselves. You can go on board and have a look around. There is information everywhere and tour guides will tell you anything you want to know.

Speedboats like this are toys for the rich and famous.

WN1384RA

FIND OUT LATER...

Which boat is the most difficult to see?

Which boat takes miles to stop?

Which boat dives the deepest?

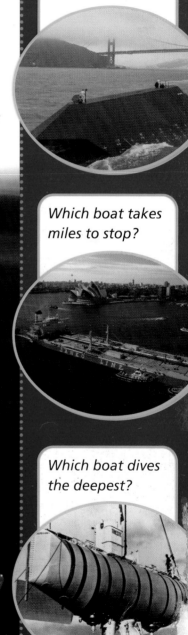

5

THE SHIPPING STORY

What turns an ordinary boat into an amazing boat? Is it speed or is it size? Must it be a record breaker? Does it have to be modern?

It could be all of these things or none of them. It is likely that the greatest boats will have something special that makes them different from the others.

Perhaps they can dive the deepest, or maybe they are the heaviest, largest, fastest or weirdest. Many of the boats that people think are the best can be found in this book.

BUILT FOR BATTLE

Nimitz-class aircraft carriers are the largest warships afloat. They have over 5500 **crew** and cost around US $5 billion to build. They are over 330 metres long, carry 85 aircraft and are powered by two nuclear reactors. They are huge!

TECH TALK

Royal Clipper: technical data
- **Masts**: 5
- Length: 143 metres
- Width: 16.5 metres
- Weight: 5000 tonnes
- Crew: 105
- Maximum mast height: 60 metres

If the sea looks too cold, the *Royal Clipper* has three on-board swimming pools!

crew   group of people who work on a boat or ship
mast   upright pole that sails are attached to

OLD MEETS NEW

The most amazing boats do not always have to be the most modern. There are many different ways to travel the oceans, after all.

The *Royal Clipper* is the world's largest sailing ship. This ship mixes modern luxury and old-fashioned, romantic charm.

Sails are not computer-operated on the *Royal Clipper*. Skilled **sailors** do the work by hand, just as they did in the old days. But the ship is built from modern materials.

UNDERWATER GIANT

This Russian Typhoon-class **submarine** is the largest sub ever built. It is 172 metres long and has a crew of 160. It can reach 46 km/h (29 mph) under water and can go 400 metres deep.

sailor member of a ship's crew
submarine ship that can travel under water

WIND POWER

Sailing uses the power of moving air to push a boat through water. People learned how to use the wind to move their boats thousands of years ago.

ANCIENT POWER

The oldest picture of a sail is from Egypt. It is nearly 8000 years old. It was a simple square sail, which can still be seen on sailing ships today. Sails allowed the ancient Greeks and the Romans to build great trading ships. Viking longships also had sails. Over the years, people learned how to make better sails. Having good sailing ships meant that a country could trade and fight successfully.

SAIL SPEED

Clipper ships were fast sailing **vessels** built to carry **cargo**. Two of the most famous are the *Cutty Sark* and the *Thermopylae*. Both ships broke speed records in the nineteenth century. The *Thermopylae*, pictured above, was destroyed in 1907. The *Cutty Sark* is now a museum and has attracted more than 15 million visitors.

HMS *Victory* was one of the most powerful sailing ships.

   dry dock   special harbour where ships can be kept out of water

RULING THE WAVES

The British were very powerful in the 18th and 19th centuries. A major reason for this was their excellent ships. HMS *Victory* was a huge, powerful gun platform that could sink any of its enemies.

Admiral Lord Nelson died on board *Victory* at the Battle of Trafalgar in 1805. *Victory* was retired in 1812. Today it is in a **dry dock** at Portsmouth, England. It attracts half-a-million visitors every year.

TECH TALK

HMS *Victory*: technical data
- Length: 69 metres
- Width: 15.7 metres
- Depth: 7.0 metres
- Highest **mast**: 62.4 metres
- Number of sails: 37
- Top speed: 19 km/h (12 mph)
- Number of guns: 104
- Crew: 821

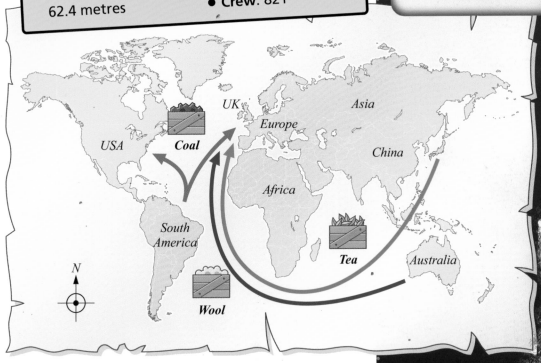

STEAM AND SPEED

During the nineteeth century, steam engines began to take the place of wind and sail power. Many inventors and engineers tried to find new mechanical ways of using steam to power ships.

PADDLE POWER

The first big change was the invention of the paddlewheel. When these huge wheels turned, the wide, flat blades dipped into the water and pushed the boat along.

BELOW DECKS

In the engine room, a coal fire heated water to produce steam. The steam ran through pipes to an engine. The steam forced a **piston** to move in and out of a **cylinder** in the engine. This piston was attached to a **crankshaft** that turned the paddlewheel.

STORMING SIRIUS

The English paddle steamer *Sirius* was the first ship to cross the Atlantic Ocean using just steam power. *Sirius* only held the **Blue Riband** for a single day in 1838, but was the first ship to make the crossing without using a sail.

The *Clermont* could easily carry up to 100 passengers.

crankshaft   part of an engine that is joined to the pistons.

TICKET TO RIDE

Paddle steamers were soon being used all over the world. They were very good on calm water such as lakes and rivers.

In 1807 the first successful steamboat company offered regular trips up and down the Hudson River between New York City and Albany in the USA.

The journey was made on the steamboat *Clermont*, built by the inventor Robert Fulton. His machine could make the 240-kilometre (150-mile) trip in 32 hours, with an average speed of around 8 km/h (5 mph).

The idea soon caught on. Paddle steamers began chugging up and down rivers all over the world. The most famous were the luxury steamers of the Mississippi River, USA. These steamers are still going strong today.

PROPELLERS FOR THE SEA

When it was built in 1843, the SS *Great Britain* was the largest ship afloat. It was designed by the famous engineer Isambard Kingdom Brunel and was the first **propeller** ship designed for the sea. A propeller ship moves using a set of underwater blades. These blades are spun round by the steam engine to produce movement.

In 1861, the SS Great Britain transported the first English cricket team to tour Australia.

cylinder   tube-shaped part of engine where fuel is burned
piston   part of engine that slides in and out of cylinder

11

BUILDING A SHIP

Many people are involved in building a ship. **Welders**, engineers, electricians, plumbers, carpenters, painters, **riveters** and blacksmiths all play their part in preparing a ship for the sea.

SHIPBUILDING YARDS

A hundred years ago, shipbuilding yards were common around the coast. Even when metal replaced wood as the main building material, people carried on building ships in much the same way. The 'skeleton' of the ship was put together first, and then metal plates were riveted to it, just like the planks used in a wooden craft.

When it was finished, the ship was launched by smashing a champagne bottle over the **bow**.

I NAME THIS SHIP...

The launch of a new ship is a spectacular and exciting event. Many people turn up to watch monster supertankers slide down into the water.

assembly   putting together different parts
bow   front end of a boat or ship

MODERN TIMES

These days, there are far fewer shipbuilding yards. Ships are no longer the only way to transport **cargo** and people around the world.

Computers are used in today's shipbuilding. Many jobs are now done by robot workers, such as metal plate-cutting and **assembly**. Ships are built in sections and are only brought to the dock for assembly. When a ship is launched today, it is often as an empty floating shell. The work of assembling the inside of the ship begins when it is actually afloat.

rivet short metal pin that fixes sheets of metal together
welder person who joins pieces of metal by melting the edges

13

LUXURY LINERS

A **liner** was a special ship, built to carry large numbers of passengers across the Atlantic and Pacific Oceans. The ships were as luxurious as the best hotels. Only the very rich could afford the luxury. For most passengers the cabins were very small and crowded.

The golden age of the liner was during the 1920s and 1930s. There was great competition between the shipping companies to provide the fastest service. The **Blue Riband** was an award for the fastest ship to cross the Atlantic. The fastest ship would become famous and get more passengers or **cargo**.

LIVING IT UP

Life aboard a luxury liner comes with many comforts. There are swimming pools, restaurants, theatres, shopping arcades and night clubs, all for the enjoyment of passengers.

The *Queen Mary* completed 1001 Atlantic crossings.

Blue Riband   award given to the fastest ship to cross the Atlantic Ocean

DEATH OF THE FLOATING PALACES

By the 1950s jet aircraft were able to cross the oceans much more quickly than ships. The great luxury liners could not compete and stopped running. Only a very small number are still running today.

HALES TROPHY

Harold Hales introduced the Hales Trophy in 1933. This is now awarded to the holder of the Blue Riband.

CAT-POWER

In 1998 the Blue Riband was awarded to a Danish super ship, *Catlink IV* (below). This ship managed an average speed of 76 km/h (47.5 mph) on the journey across the Atlantic.

▶▶▶▶▶▶▶▶▶▶

Find out more about the history of the Blue Riband on pages 58–59.

liner   big ship that carries passengers all over the world

WAR AT SEA

At the beginning of the twentieth century, Britain had the world's most powerful navy. Even though World War I was mainly a land war, the Royal Navy ruled the seas. This meant that supplies could be easily carried to support the land army. Having sea power made a country very strong.

DREADNOUGHT

Built in 1906, HMS *Dreadnought* changed warfare at sea forever. It was the fastest and best-armed warship in the world. Its closest rivals did not have half its firepower. It made all other battleships out of date.

BATTLESHIP GIANTS

By the start of World War II in 1939, many countries had produced some awesome battleships. The British navy had HMS *Hood* and HMS *King George V*. The USA had the USS *Iowa* and the USS *North Carolina*. The German navy fought back with the *Bismarck*, *Scharnhorst* and the *Graf Spee*.

This cruise missile is being fired by a US battleship.

UP TO SPEED   nuclear missile   weapon with huge destructive power

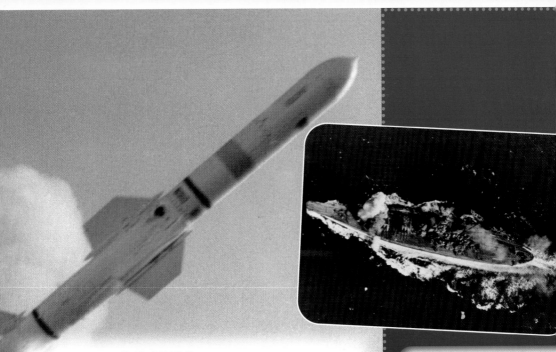

CHANGING ROLES

World War II signalled a change in the role of the battleship. When Japanese planes sank eight US battleships that were docked at Pearl Harbor in 1941, it was clear how important aircraft could be. The days of great battleships fighting to rule the waves were ending.

A NEW ROLE

The invention of **nuclear missiles** meant that wars could be fought in a different way. Large, expensive battleships were no longer so important. Many were taken out of service and scrapped. Today, battleships no longer fight each other at sea and there are very few left. The firepower of smaller modern ships is much greater and they can now do the job of the battleships.

JAPANESE GIANT

The Japanese battleship *Yamato* was the largest ever built. Its main guns were the largest to go to sea. Each shell they fired weighed 1460 kilograms, about the weight of a large car. Even though it had more armour than any other ship afloat, the *Yamato* was sunk by US forces in 1945.

FLAT TOPS

The most powerful warships afloat are the huge aircraft carriers, more commonly known as 'flat tops'.

Aircraft are very important in modern warfare. But for aircraft to be useful, they must have a safe place to take off and land.

TO BOLDLY GO...

The first nuclear-powered aircraft carrier was the USS *Enterprise*, launched in 1961. It carries 90 aircraft and has a **crew** of more than 5500. This super ship can go for 15 years without having to refuel.

FLOATING AIRPORTS

Aircraft carriers can go anywhere in the world. They act as a base for military operations. Wherever there is a problem, aircraft carriers are usually the first on the scene. **Reconnaissance** aircraft can be launched from their decks. These planes bring back the information that ships' commanders need.

Aircraft carriers can be up to 350 metres long.

ONE SHIP, MANY JOBS

Aircraft can be launched to attack enemy targets. Because the largest flat tops carry as many as 90 aircraft, these attacks can be awesome, causing incredible damage and destruction. Aircraft carriers also launch landing craft filled with troops during invasions.

Aircraft carriers are used for many other operations. They often look after medical helicopters and make sure that troops are kept fully supplied with everything they need. They also defend against air attacks with missiles and helicopters. They even carry special helicopters designed to seek out and destroy **submarines**.

A flat top is also a command centre. In times of trouble and danger, the big decisions are made on board.

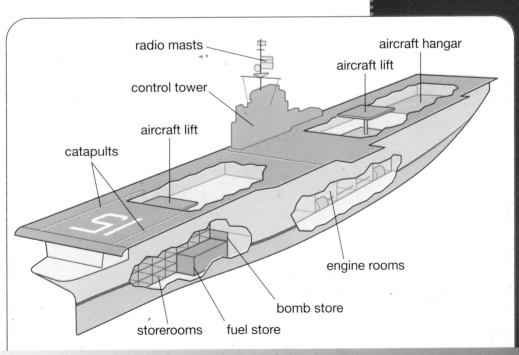

radio masts

control tower

aircraft lift

catapults

aircraft hangar

aircraft lift

engine rooms

bomb store

storerooms   fuel store

19

HIGH-SPEED NAVY

By far the fastest military boats are the hydrofoils and hovercraft. Both of these are so quick because they sail with their **hulls** above the water.

The advantages of a military hydrofoil are clear. They are much faster than normal ships. Hovercraft are very fast, too, and can be used in many different situations.

ANY BEACH, ANYWHERE

Hovercraft are not used far out in open seas. Their main use is around the coast. They are used to get troops quickly on to the land. As hovercraft can operate on land, troops and equipment do not have to be unloaded at the water's edge.

JETS

Launched in 1967, the *Tucumcari* was the first hydrofoil to use water jets instead of **propellers**. It was used during the Vietnam war and could travel at around 96 km/h (60 mph).

> ❯❯❯❯❯❯❯❯❯❯❯
>
> To find out more about hovercraft, see pages 34–35.

drag   (also called water resistance) force that pushes against a boat and slows it down as it moves through the water

ON PATROL

Smaller hovercraft are excellent coastal and river patrol boats. They are not only used in wartime. They also help in anti-smuggling and anti-piracy operations. They are quick and **manoeuvrable**. As they are not just limited to the water, they can patrol the land too.

The larger assault hovercraft carry huge loads but still travel at around 80 km/h (50 mph). They are also well armed and can fight off most attackers. This has led to them being nicknamed 'hovertanks'. Some assault hovercraft have even been used in the middle of the desert.

HOW HYDROFOILS WORK

A hydrofoil is simply an aircraft wing attached underneath a ship. When the ship reaches a certain speed, the wing creates enough lift to push the craft up out of the water. This means less **drag** and faster speeds.

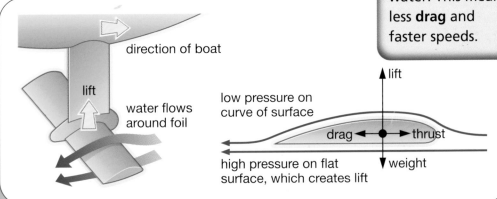

direction of boat

lift

water flows around foil

low pressure on curve of surface

lift

drag ← ● → thrust

weight

high pressure on flat surface, which creates lift

Hovercraft are effective on land as well as water.

hull main body of a ship that sits in the water
manoeuvrable able to move and turn easily

INVISIBLE ATTACKER

Surprise is a great weapon in sea warfare, but ships can be spotted easily by **radar**. The best answer is to design a ship that is hard for radar to see. If a ship is the right shape and covered with the right materials, radar is useless. These invisible craft are called stealth ships.

TESTING AT SEA

The Lockheed-Martin *Sea Shadow* is a stealth ship. It was originally used to test new technology, but it became clear that its stealth features were the most important. It is now in full service with the US Navy.

DISAPPEARING...

How the *Sea Shadow* becomes 'invisible':

- slanted surfaces deflect radar
- **hull** is made of special material that is hard for radar to see
- twin hulls create a small **wake** and little noise
- engines are very quiet.

TECH TALK

Sea Shadow: technical data
- Length: 50 metres
- Width: 20.7 metres
- Weight: 569 tonnes
- Crew: 10

radar   (RAdio Detection And Ranging) way of detecting things when they are many miles away

SECRET MISSION

The *Sea Shadow* was designed and built in complete secrecy. Parts were made in different places and by different teams of engineers. This was so that information about the ship could be kept as secret as possible. Even today, only very basic information about this ship can be found.

Sea Shadow is the secret agent of the ship world. It is outstanding at **reconnaissance** missions and avoiding being seen by its enemies.

SILENT AND DEADLY

This Swedish Visby-class ship is built for anti-**submarine** warfare. It is powered by quiet water-jet engines and has a light **carbon-fibre** hull that is invisible to radar and **sonar**. All its weapons are carried inside the hull.

wake   waves that spread out from the back of a ship when it is moving forward

BENEATH THE WAVES

Water covers 71 per cent of the Earth's surface. Ships have sailed over every part of it. But the ocean beneath the surface is largely unexplored. Even though more than 90 per cent of life on our planet lives in the sea, we know very little about it.

DEEPEST DIVE

The deeper you go, the more unexplored the waters become. The deepest place in the world is in the Pacific. It is called Challenger Deep, after the ship that found it. Mount Everest could sit in Challenger Deep and still easily be covered with about 2 kilometres (1.2 miles) of water.

Sending **submarines** as deep as this is very difficult and very dangerous.

BATHYSPHERE

Dr William Beebe invented the Bathysphere in 1930. It was a large metal container that held air and he used it for diving. He dived to a depth of 923 metres in it. The previous record was by a diver in an armoured suit at just 160 metres. Beebe explored where no other human had been.

To withstand the pressure of the water, the walls of the Bathysphere were 45 cm thick.

24

THE DEEPEST EVER

In 1960 the US Navy sent a specially designed mini-submarine to Challenger Deep. It was called the *Trieste*, and two men went down inside it.

At 10,616 metres below the surface the *Trieste* touched the bottom.

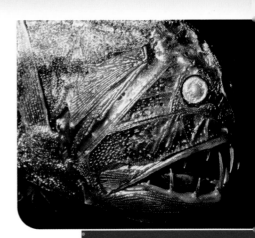

MIGHTY-MINI

The *Trieste* may have been tiny, but it had to be very strong. The deeper a submarine goes, the more water is on top of it. This means that there is a greater pressure pushing down. Imagine how incredibly strong the pressure is with 11 kilometres (nearly 7 miles) of water above you!

The *Trieste* holds the record for the deepest dive to this day. It will continue to hold it unless somewhere deeper is found.

STRANGE FISH

Some very weird creatures live in the deep ocean. Because of the darkness, their eyes are very large. They often have long fangs and look more like creatures from another planet. Some fish can even light up.

air trapped inside

DIVING BELLS

Turn a glass tumbler upside down and lower it into a bowl of water. The air stays inside the glass. Diving bells work in the same way, but are large enough to contain people. They have been used for centuries, but people think the English scientist Roger Bacon invented them in 1250.

ROBOT WRECK-FINDERS

When ships sink, they go to the bottom of the ocean. Depending on where they are, that can be a long way down. Scientists use amazing technology to find and study shipwrecks.

Scientists use **sonar** to find shipwrecks. Then they send remote **infrared** cameras down to check. The cameras can be 'driven' to wherever the operator wants.

The most dangerous and expensive method scientists use to study wrecks is to go down and have a look themselves. This is done in specially designed craft called submersibles. The most famous submersible is called *Alvin*.

infrared type of light that cannot be seen by the human eye

LOST AND FOUND

This amazing submersible has underwater lights, cameras and robotic arms to collect samples.

Alvin has had an exciting life so far. As well as searching for wrecks all over the world, *Alvin* even helped to recover a lost nuclear bomb. But its most famous adventure was finding the *Titanic*, the cruise liner that sank in 1912.

TECH TALK

Alvin: technical data
- Length: 7.1 metres
- Height: 3.7 metres
- Operating depth: 4500 metres
- Crew: 3
- Normal dive length: 6–10 hours
- Maximum life support: 72 hours

UNSINKABLE?

The most famous shipping disaster in history happened in 1912. The luxury cruise **liner** *Titanic* set off on its **maiden voyage** to the USA. The proud owners boasted that it was unsinkable. They were wrong. *Titanic* hit an iceberg and hundreds died. This picture of the front of the *Titanic* was taken by *Alvin* more than 70 years after it sank.

sonar (SOund and NAvigation Ranging) method of detecting where things are underwater

Ohio-class submarine: technical data

- Length: 170 metres
- Width: 12.8 metres
- Top speed: 27 km/h (17 mph) (surface); 46.5 km/h (29 mph) (under water)
- Crew: 160

NUCLEAR SUBS

A nuclear **submarine** is powered by a nuclear reactor. It can stay at sea for very long periods of time, as it does not need to be refuelled. Submarines are the original stealth ships. They cruise the oceans of the world unseen and carry out a wide range of missions.

FICTION INTO FACT

The first nuclear submarine was the USS *Nautilus*, seen below. It was named after the fictional submarine from Jules Verne's story *20,000 Leagues Under the Sea*. *Nautilus* was launched in 1954 and soon broke all underwater speed and distance records. In 1958 it was the first ship to reach the North Pole, deep below the surface, of course.

OHIO CLASS

There are at least sixteen of these submarines in service. Each one carries enough nuclear missiles to destroy entire continents.

28   **UP TO SPEED**   ballistic missile   explosive rocket that has its own engines and can direct itself towards a chosen target

MODERN SUBMARINES

There are two different types of modern submarine.

Attack submarines hunt down and destroy surface ships and other submarines. They can stay under water for years because the air inside them is recycled. They can stay at sea for a long time, so they carry many weapons. This means they do not have to return home to collect more.

The second type is the **ballistic missile** craft. These do not fight other ships, but travel the oceans, staying hidden. When needed, they rise from the seas to launch **nuclear missiles** at an enemy. They are the most deadly fighting machines ever built.

TECH TALK

Attack sub classes:

USA
   Virginia
   Los Angeles
Russia
   Akula
   OSCAR
UK
   Astute
   Trafalgar

Ballistic sub classes:

USA
   Ohio
Russia
   Typhoon
UK
   Vanguard

The USS *Nautilus* is now a floating museum in Connecticut, USA.

SHIPPING WORLD

Ships are still the most important way to transport **cargo** around the globe. About 95 per cent of all goods travel by sea.

CONTAINERS

Cargo is packed into standard-sized containers. Giant cranes lift the sealed containers straight off the ships on to lorries waiting below. Although this has made cargo handling simpler, some ships are so big that some ports cannot cope with them.

GIANT TANKERS

Oil tankers are special ships that carry oil around the world. Without them the world would not be able to operate in the way it does today. As we use enormous amounts of oil every day, the ships that carry the oil are huge.

ENVIRONMENTAL NIGHTMARE

Oil tankers have a huge environmental responsibility. If things go wrong there can be a disaster. The tanker above, the *Torrey Canyon*, hit rocks in the English Channel in 1967. The oil spill caused terrible damage to the water and coastline.

MONSTER

The Norwegian *Jahre Viking* is the largest ship afloat. This oil tanker is massive. It is so big that it takes several kilometres for it to slow down and stop.

The *Jahre Viking* is 458 metres long. If you could tip the *Jahre Viking* on its end, the ship would be taller than the Empire State Building in New York. In fact, its cargo holds are so big they could swallow up St Paul's Cathedral four times over. If the Eiffel Tower was laid on its side, that would fit in, too.

Each time the *Jahre Viking* goes to sea, it is carrying cargo worth around US $150 million. The **crew** of this monster use bicycles to move about on deck.

COMPUTER CONTROL

Ships must be very carefully loaded to keep them **stable**. Cargo is carefully positioned using computers. If the ship does not sit evenly in the water, it may be in trouble once its journey has started.

MEGALINERS

Luxury **liners** had their golden age in the early twentieth century. Their main purpose then was taking passengers from one place to another. There are far fewer liners around today. They now take people on luxury cruise holidays.

COMFORT AND STYLE

To take a holiday cruise is many people's idea of the ultimate in luxury. The ships sail to some of the most beautiful and exciting places on Earth, while the lucky passengers enjoy all that these amazing luxury **vessels** have to offer.

The best liners have restaurants, theatres and shopping arcades on board. There are even health and beauty clubs and 'street cafés'. There are many different kinds of entertainment, and there is always something to do or see.

TECH TALK

Voyager of the Seas: **technical data**

- Length: 311 metres
- Width: 48 metres
- Cruising speed: 40 km/h (25 mph)
- Crew: 1181
- Weight: 137,000 tonnes
- Passengers: 3840

VOYAGER OF THE SEAS

When it put to sea in 1999, the *Voyager of the Seas* was the largest cruise ship afloat. This amazing ship has a skating rink, a street fair and a rock-climbing wall. There is also a casino, theatre, cinema, library, chapel and several nightclubs. Sports fans can play golf, basketball, volleyball, go scuba diving or go to the gym. You can also eat in a different restaurant every night of your holiday!

FIT FOR A QUEEN

The world's most famous cruise liner is the *Queen Elizabeth II*, or the *QE2* for short. It was first launched in 1969, and even has a branch of the famous Harrods store on board.

◄ ◄ ◄ ◄ ◄ ◄ ◄ ◄ ◄ ◄
To find out more about luxury liners, see pages 14–15.

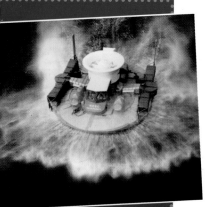

HOVERCRAFT

Hovercraft are ships that float over water and land on a cushion of air. The British scientist Christopher Cockerell invented the hovercraft in 1956.

EARLY DAYS

Cockerell tried out his first ideas using cat food and coffee tins, a huge fan and some kitchen scales! Some of the early **prototypes** looked very strange. But Cockerell learned that travelling on air could be done.

FIRST TO SUCCEED

The first real working hovercraft was the *SRN1*. Many scientists thought that a hovercraft was possible, but Cockerell's *SRN1* was the first to successfully operate in 1959.

◄ ◄ ◄ ◄ ◄ ◄ ◄ ◄ ◄
To find out more about hovercraft, see pages 20–21.

Cockerell's idea went on to become amazingly successful.

prototype   version that is built and tested before the real thing is made

THE AIR CUSHION

The engine of a hovercraft runs massive fans that blow air. The air is forced under a rubber skirt around the boat. The air pushes the boat up so it 'floats'.

Hovercraft are not slowed by **drag,** which means they can reach very high speeds. The fastest military hovercraft can top 160 km/h (100 mph).

Today the larger hovercraft are used less often for carrying passengers and **cargo.** Now hovercraft are mainly used on a much smaller scale by the military or emergency services. Single-seat hovercraft racing is also a popular sport.

WORLD'S BIGGEST

The British *SRN4* (Mark 3) is the world's largest hovercraft. It weighs 305 tonnes and has a top speed of over 120 km/h (75 mph). It can carry 60 cars and 418 passengers across the English Channel. But hovercraft are expensive to run and are being replaced by Seacats. These are slower, but on a short run the difference is not that important.

TECH TALK

Many of the hovercraft that are used to carry passengers do not get a chance to travel at full power due to safety reasons. They are capable of going much faster than ferries.

hovercraft

SEACATS

The fastest powerboats and yachts have two **hulls** rather than one. These ships are called **catamarans**. The largest catamarans on the water today are the Seacats.

FAST FERRIES

The Seacats are a range of super-quick ferries. They were the world's first catamarans to carry cars and lorries. Seacats are nearly twice as fast as ordinary ferries. They also give smooth rides in rough water.

TWICE AS GOOD

A Seacat's two hulls are narrow, and are made from aluminium. This design helps them to reach much higher speeds than ordinary ferries.

TECH TALK

Super Seacat: technical data
- Length: 100 metres
- Width: 17.1 metres
- Height: 10.7 metres
- Maximum speed: 75 km/h (47 mph)
- Maximum passengers: 800
- Maximum cars: 175

catamaran   boat with two hulls

FASTER AND SMOOTHER

As the Seacat powers along, huge waterjet engines lift its two hulls high in the water. This is why the ride seems smooth even when the seas are rough.

To reach very high speeds, the engines spin up to 750 times a minute. This sucks water up into the water jets. This water is then blasted out again, thrusting the craft forward. The **wake** created by these jets is massive.

The Seacats are very sporty-looking for a ferry. They were designed by the same Italian company that shaped Ferrari sports cars, so this is not surprising!

RECORD BREAKER

A Seacat broke the record for the fastest crossing of the Atlantic Ocean in 1990. It won the Hales Trophy after crossing the ocean in 3 days, 7 hours and 54 minutes.

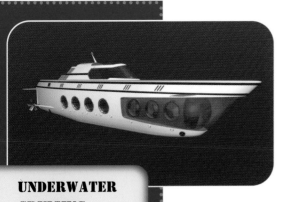

LUXURY YACHTS

For the super-rich, owning a luxury **yacht** is the ultimate symbol of wealth. They come in many shapes and sizes but they all have one thing in common: luxury beyond belief!

UNDERWATER CRUISING

At 36 metres long, the *Seattle 1000* is a **submarine** super yacht. Not only does it sail on the surface with every possible comfort and luxury, it can also dive to a depth of 305 metres. Windows allow passengers to watch underwater life.

FLOATING HOTELS

Smaller luxury yachts are often known as motor-sailers. They can be powered by sails, like a traditional yacht. They also have engines in case the wind dies down. They normally carry between five and ten people.

The larger luxury yachts are really motor yachts, as they can only get their power from an engine. The largest can look after as many as 60 guests.

The *Lady Moura* is one of the largest yachts in the world.

STYLE

As you might expect, inside these craft no expense is spared. Everything is made from top quality materials and uses all the latest equipment. There is plenty of deck space to soak up the sun and the sights, too!

BUY OR HIRE?

Many companies hire out their luxury yachts for very wealthy people to use for holidays. A private jet collects the holidaymaker from wherever they choose. Then a luxury car carries them to the harbour. The captain and **crew** are waiting to greet them. If you have many millions to spare, you could buy your own luxury yacht!

PREDATOR PERFECTION

The outside of the Sunseeker *Predator* is a racing machine; the inside is a palace. The *Predator* is so expensive that only a few are made each year. Only very rich people can afford to own them.

BREAKING THE ICE

In very cold parts of the world, special ships are needed to break the ice that can form on waterways. These ships are called icebreakers.

Icebreakers do the important job of making sure that ports and harbours stay open in winter. They clear the way for other ships. They can also be used on rescue and exploration missions.

BRUTE FORCE

The early icebreakers were made out of wood. They tried to batter their way through the ice using brute force. Because wood is quite flexible, these ships had some success. But the strength of the ice always won in the end.

INTELLIGENT DESIGN

Modern icebreakers are computer-designed to help them beat the ice. The **hull** has a stepped design, which helps it to rise above the ice. The whole weight of the ship can then press down like a giant sledgehammer.

The hull of an icebreaker is extremely thick. It is made of special steel that stays strong even at low temperatures. Inside the hull is a skeleton of thick steel ribs. These stop the ice from crushing the ship like a tin can.

BATTERING RAM

The engines of an icebreaker are powerful. Some are even nuclear-powered. They must force the ship up against the ice. As the engines drive the hull up and forward, gravity does the hard work of smashing the ice.

SEASONAL ICE-SMASHER

The *Botnica* is three ships in one. In summer it can operate as a towboat or as a supply ship. In winter it returns to duty as an icebreaker. It keeps the **coast** and waterways of Finland open for business.

SMALL BOATS

James Bond films have been thrilling audiences since 1962. They are among the film world's most popular action-adventure films. All the films involve Bond in stunning chase scenes. Many of these action-packed chases involve boats.

As the character of James Bond was a commander in the Royal Navy, it is only right that many of his adventures should happen on water.

AWESOME STUNTS

Live and Let Die includes a spectacular chase scene involving speedboats. The boats jump over roads, hurtle over roadblocks, cut corners by going on dry land and even gatecrash a wedding party.

BOND ON THE WATER

In *Thunderball*, Bond chases the *Disco Volante*. This unique ship splits in two during the action to reveal a hydrofoil. There are also amazing underwater action scenes in this film, using specially designed underwater craft.

This Lotus could travel on land and on water.

gondola   long, narrow, flat-bottomed boat used on canals; it is moved along by pushing on a long pole.

SUPER BOATS FOR A SUPER HERO

The Spy Who Loved Me sees plenty of action in boats, too. Most famous is the Lotus Esprit submarine car that comes straight out of the sea on to a crowded beach. This film also features the *Liparus*, a tanker that swallows other ships, as well as the sight of Bond on a ski-bike.

In *Tomorrow Never Dies*, Bond has to track down a stealth boat to defeat the villain. Once he finds the stealth boat, he must somehow get on board.

Moonraker mixes action with a sense of humour. Bond used a specially equipped **gondola** to get the better of his enemies.

BOND'S BEST?
The 'Q boat' (below) is the best-equipped Bond boat so far. In *The World Is Not Enough*, Bond puts it to use on the River Thames. The boat can dive under water and run on land!

POWERBOATS

Racing powerboats are designed to win. Speed and strength are more important than comfort or space. There are three main types of powerboat.

HULL DESIGN

Powerboats with a single hull have a narrow, v-shaped **bow**. This hull is designed to rise up on top of the water at high speeds. The hulls are flat underneath so they skim the surface with very little **drag**.

CLASS-1 POWERBOATS

These are the fastest racing boats on the water. Two massive engines take up over half the space of the 4.5-tonne craft. **Crews** of two compete around courses that are about 250 kilometres (160 miles) long. They must make their way around specially placed **buoys** at speeds of up to 240 km/h (150 mph).

These powerboats are spectacular and very noisy. It is also a dangerous sport, so the crew rides inside a **cockpit** as strong as those on fighter jet!

buoy floating sign or marker that acts as a warning to ships
cockpit small space in a racing boat where the crew sit

CLASS-2 POWERBOATS

These boats are slightly smaller than Class-1s. They include both single **hulls** and **catamarans**.

The **monohulls** do better in rough conditions, but the catamarans are better in smooth conditions. This is because the catamarans need smooth water to skim across. A monohull cuts through the waves, so smooth conditions are not so important.

CIRCUIT RACERS

Circuit racers are small, single-seaters that race around short, tight circuits. There can be as many as 70 laps in a race. Circuit racing takes place close to land, so many people turn up to watch.

The cornering is spectacular. Sharp turns are taken at over 144 km/h (90 mph), which puts more pressure on the driver than on a pilot in a fighter jet!

POWER CATS

The two slim hulls of a catamaran cut through water faster than large single hulls. Catamarans roll from side to side less than a monohull. A cushion of air between the hulls lifts the boat, so it looks like it is flying.

monohull ship with a single hull

SUPER-SAIL CRAFT

The fastest sailing craft are the big ocean racers. The **monohull** yachts can cope with the roughest oceans and the strongest winds. The **catamaran** ocean racers can reach higher top speeds.

SAVING WEIGHT

In races or record attempts, it is important to keep weight low. The **crew** only have one set of clothes and inside the boat is almost empty, apart from **hammocks** to sleep in. All the food is dried to save weight and a machine turns seawater into drinking water.

A number of things are required to win races and break records. The yacht must be well designed, strong and tough. The crew must be experts. Finally, some luck is needed to make sure the wind is helpful.

hammock   piece of cloth that hangs above the floor, used as a bed.

RECORD BREAKER

The catamaran *Club Med* broke many sailing records in 2000. It crossed the Atlantic Ocean in 10 days, 14 hours, 54 minutes and 43 seconds. That is nearly two days faster than the old record for a wind-powered ship.

Club Med also broke the record for the longest distance sailed in a single day. It travelled 1001.1 kilometres (625.7 miles) in 24 hours. The average speed of the yacht was 41.6 km/h (26 mph).

TECH TALK

Ocean-racing catamaran: technical data
- Weight: 10 tonnes
- Length: 27 metres
- Width: 13 metres
- Mast height: 31 metres
- Crew: 11
- Top speed: 64 km/h (40 mph)

ROUND THE WORLD

Every four years, the top ocean-racing yachts take part in the Whitbread Round the World Race. It is the most difficult of all sailing races. The yachts race nearly 51,200 kilometres (32,000 miles). It takes them eight months to finish the race.

WATER-SPEED RECORD

Speed records are there to be broken. People are always trying to be 'The Fastest'. Breaking the water-speed record is very risky, because it is more dangerous to race on water than on land.

THE BLUEBIRD LEGEND

Vehicles called *Bluebird* have held many speed records, on both water and land. In the 1930s, Sir Malcolm Campbell broke nine land-speed records and three water-speed records. Every car or boat he used was called *Bluebird*.

LIKE FATHER, LIKE SON

In 1964 Campbell's son, Donald, decided to follow in his father's footsteps. He broke the land-speed record in Australia. Of course, this 648-km/h (403-mph) car was called *Bluebird*.

HOME-MADE

Ken Warby broke the water-speed record in 1978 in *Spirit of Australia*. He built it himself using a second-hand aeroplane engine that he bought for US $65. He reached a speed of 507 km/h (317 mph).

This picture was taken seconds before the crash that killed Donald Campell.

SUCCESS, THEN DISASTER

Donald Campbell became the only man to hold land- and water-speed records at the same time. He had achieved something his father did not. But in 1967 he wanted to be the first person to go over 480 km/h (300 mph) on water. He took *Bluebird* to Lake Coniston in England.

Campbell tried to break the record without waiting for waves on the water to settle. As he reached top speed, *Bluebird* hit a wave and lifted out of the water. It spun several times in the air and slammed into the water. Donald Campbell's body was not found until 2001 – 34 years later.

Sir Malcolm Campbell in *Bluebird K4*.

➤ ➤ ➤ ➤ ➤ ➤ ➤ ➤ ➤ ➤

Find out more about the water-speed record on pages 58–59.

SPECIAL SHIPS

The Boeing Sea-Launch programme is designed to launch rockets into space from the middle of the ocean. These rockets carry **satellites**. Modern technology relies heavily upon satellites circling the Earth.

LAUNCHING FROM THE SEA

There are advantages of sending a rocket into space from the ocean. The main one is that the rocket can be launched from the **equator**. This means the rocket will be taking the shortest, most direct route into orbit. Launching satellites this way is also cheaper.

The *Odyssey* arrives at the port of Long Beach on October 4, 1998. The first launch was in March, 1999.

equator   imaginary line around the middle of the Earth, halfway between the North and South Poles

LAUNCH PAD

The launch platform is called *Odyssey*. It is similar to an oil rig. It has space for the 68 **crew** and technicians as well as the rocket and launch system itself. The platform is 133 metres long, 67 metres wide and weighs more than 50,000 tonnes.

COMMAND CENTRE

The Assembly and Command Ship (ACS) sails around the launch platform. The countdown is controlled from the ACS.

Many successful rocket launches have taken place from the middle of the ocean. Many more will happen in the future.

ROCKETS

Zenit 3SL rockets are used by the Sea-Launch system. They are 60 metres long and 4 metres wide. They use liquid oxygen as a fuel. The different parts of the rocket are made all over the world. They are put together on board the ACS.

satellite   device that circles the Earth, sending and receiving signals

WIG BOATS

A WIG boat is a cross between a hovercraft and an aircraft. WIG stands for Wing In Ground-effect. WIG boats skim across the surface of the water at very high speeds. They have been experimental for many years and no one has quite managed to make them widely used.

GROUND EFFECT

When an aircraft lands, just before touchdown, it seems like the plane does not want to go lower. Air becomes trapped between the wing and the runway, forming an air cushion. A WIG boat uses this cushion to ride upon.

The problem has been that WIG boats need to reach high speeds to make this effect happen.

NEW MONSTER?

The aircraft maker Boeing is designing a new WIG boat. Although little is known about this craft, it is said to be bigger than the Caspian Sea Monster and will be used for carrying **cargo**. When it travels at 7 metres above the water it should reach 480 km/h (300 mph).

CIA US Government agency set up to gather information about potential enemies

THE CASPIAN SEA MONSTER

The largest WIG craft ever built was the giant Russian *Ekranoplan*. It was very secret and was first learned about by the CIA in the 1960s. They nicknamed it the Caspian Sea Monster.

Ekranoplan was more than 92 metres long. It was designed as a military **vessel** for carrying between 800 and 900 soldiers. It could reach speeds of 552 km/h (345 mph) even though it weighed 540 tons. This was twice the weight of the heaviest aircraft at the time. To get up enough speed to leave the surface of the water, *Ekranoplan* had no fewer than ten engines.

ORLYONOK

The *Orlyonok* is a **prototype** designed to become a military transport craft. Early tests were successful, but the project was put on hold in 1993. New interest in WIG machines means that the *Orlyonok* may fly/sail again.

The *Ekranoplan* project was scrapped in the 1980s after a crash.

53

WEIRD IDEAS

Many strange boat designs have appeared over the years. Not all of them have been successful. Here are just a few.

FIRE AND WATER

Fire ships are an unusual but successful idea. They are really just floating fire engines, able to tackle fires on ships, or close to rivers or ports. The **hull** of a fire ship has special pumps that suck in water, then hoses spray it all over the fire. A fire ship has a nearly endless supply of water.

THE FLIP SHIP

FLIP is a weird research ship. It has doors in the floor, windows in the ceiling, tables bolted to walls and stairs that lead nowhere.

This is because *FLIP* lives up to its name. It flips on its end so only a small part is left above the surface. The weird design means that most of the ship is below the waves. This provides scientists with a much more **stable** place to carry out their research than on a bobbing ship. The waves have less effect because the ship is so well balanced under water.

SEASICK SHIP

The inventor and engineer Henry Bessemer designed a ship he hoped would cure his seasickness. The idea was to produce a platform that would always be stable, no matter how rough the sea. It was a disaster and sank on its first voyage.

Fires on board tankers can be disastrous.

FUTURE BOATS

So what does the future hold for the world of boats?

Although boats have been built for thousands of years, people are still producing new boat designs, new engines and improved building materials. The ideas never seem to run out.

SHAPING THE FUTURE

The Russian navy has developed a rocket-powered torpedo, called the Shkval. It can travel at five times the speed of a normal torpedo, over 480 km/h (300 mph). This makes it very difficult to stop.

The torpedo runs so fast because it produces millions of small bubbles around its nose. These bubbles reduce the **friction**, so a higher speed is reached with the same amount of power. Adding a rocket engine helps, too!

SUPERSONIC SUB?

Scientists hope that ideas from the Shkval torpedo could produce a supersonic submarine one day. They intend to surround a submarine with a giant bubble. This would remove most of the underwater **drag**, allowing very high speeds.

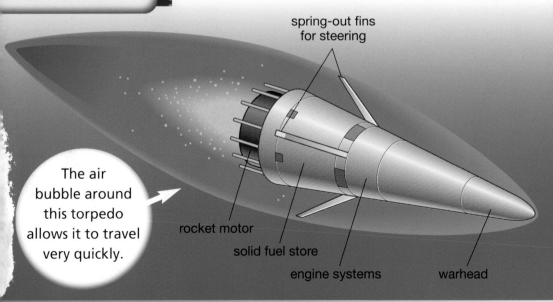

spring-out fins
for steering

The air bubble around this torpedo allows it to travel very quickly.

rocket motor

solid fuel store

engine systems

warhead

friction   force that acts when two things rub together.

NEW DESIGNS, NEW IDEAS

The technology used to design the Shkval torpedo could also be used to build super-fast **submarines**. Perhaps in the future, it will be quicker to travel under the water than on the surface.

UNDERWATER FLYING

Deep Flight is a brand new submarine design. Normal submarines rely on letting air in and out to dive and rise to the surface. A hot-air balloon rises and falls in a similar way. *Deep Flight* does not have to do this. Small wings allow the sub to 'fly' around the ocean. *Deep Flight* can change direction or depth without letting air in or out.

FASTER AND FASTER

Normal ships have a long, thin **stern** that sinks into the water. A new design called *FastShip*, above, has a wide, hollow stern. This means *FastShip* lifts up at the back and moves faster. Water jets give the ship its power.

stern   back of a boat or ship

BOAT FACTS

Water-speed record highlights				
			Speed	
Date	**Driver**	**Vehicle**	**km/h**	**mph**
1928	George Wood	Miss America VII	149.3	92.8
1930	Henry Segrave	Miss England II	159.0	98.8
1931	Gar Wood	Miss America IX	164.4	102.2
1937	Malcolm Campbell	Bluebird K3	203.2	126.3
1939	Malcolm Campbell	Bluebird K4	228.0	141.7
1950	Stanley Sayres	Slo-Mo-Shun IV	258.0	160.3
1955	Donald Campbell	Bluebird K7	325.6	202.3
1959	Donald Campbell	Bluebird K7	419.1	260.4
1967	Lee A. Taylor	Hustler	459.0	285.2
1978	Ken Warby	Spirit of Australia	511.1	317.6

Largest cruise ships		
Ship	**Weight (tonnes)**	**Passengers**
Queen Mary 2	142,200	2800
Explorer of the Seas	137,308	3840
Adventure of the Seas	137,276	3840
Mariner of the Seas	137,276	3840
Navigator of the Seas	137,276	3807
Voyager of the Seas	137,276	3840
Diamond Princess	113,000	2600
Sapphire Princess	113,000	3100
Carnival Conquest	110,239	3783
Carnival Glory	110,000	3783
Carnival Valor	110,000	3783
Crown Princess	110,000	3100

Worst oil tanker spills

Tanker	Date	Spillage (tonnes)
Atlantic Empress	July 1979	287,000
ABT Summer	May 1991	260,000
Castillo de Bellver	August 1983	252,000
Amoco Cadiz	March 1978	223,000
Haven	April 1991	144,000
Odyssey	November 1988	132,000
Torrey Canyon	March 1967	119,000
Sea Star	December 1972	115,000
Irenes Serenade	February 1980	100,000
Urquida	May 1976	100,000

Blue Riband holders

Ship	Date	Time
Sirius	1838	18 days, 14 hours, 22 minutes
Great Western	1838	12 days, 16 hours, 24 minutes
Persia	1856	8 days, 23 hours, 19 minutes
Kaiser Wilhelm	1897	5 days, 17 hours, 23 minutes
Mauretania	1909	4 days, 10 hours, 51 minutes
Queen Mary	1938	3 days, 20 hours, 42 minutes
United States	1952	3 days, 10 hours, 40 minutes
Hoverspeed Great Britain	1990	3 days, 7 hours, 54 minutes
Catlink IV	1998	2 days, 20 hours, 9 minutes

The most expensive ticket on the maiden voyage of the Queen Mary 2 in January, 2004 cost US $37,499.

There were 3547 passengers on the Titanic when it sank in 1912. There were only enough lifeboats for 1178 people.

FIND OUT MORE

ORGANIZATIONS

USS NAUTILUS
The website for the museum based in Connecticut, USA. Photos of the inside of the first nuclear submarine, and details of its history.
ussnautilus.org

HMS VICTORY
This site gives a clear idea of what it was like to live on an eighteenth-century warship.
hms-victory.com

BBC SCIENCE
Website packed with games and quizzes to find out about all aspects of science.
bbc.co.uk/science

BOOKS

Superboats, Ian Graham (Heinemann, 2003)
High-Speed Boats, S. Bornhoft (Franklin Watts, 1999)
Super Subs, David Jefferis (Crabtree Publishing, 2001)

WORLD WIDE WEB

If you want to find out more about boats you can search the Internet using keywords like these:

- 'yacht racing'
- powerboat + race
- luxury + yacht
- navy
- tanker + disaster

Make your own keywords using headings or words from this book. The search tips opposite will help you find the most useful websites.

SEARCH TIPS

There are billions of pages on the Internet so it can be difficult to find exactly what you are looking for. If you just type in 'boat' on a search engine like Google, you will get a list of 12 million web pages. These search skills will help you to find useful websites more quickly.

- Use simple keywords, not whole sentences
- Use two to six keywords in a search
- Be precise – only use names of people, places or things
- If you want to find words that go together, put quote marks around them – for example, 'world-speed record'
- Use the advanced section of your search engine
- Use the + sign between keywords to find pages with all these words.

WHERE TO SEARCH

SEARCH ENGINE

A search engine looks through the entire web and lists all sites that match the search words. The best matches are at the top of the list, on the first page. Try bbc.co.uk/search

SEARCH DIRECTORY

A search directory is like a library of websites. You can search by keyword or subject and browse through the different sites like you look through books on a library shelf. A good example is yahooligans.com

GLOSSARY

assembly/assemble putting together different parts

ballistic missile explosive rocket that has its own engines and can direct itself towards a chosen target

Blue Riband award given to the fastest ship to cross the Atlantic Ocean

bow front end of a boat or ship

buoy floating sign or marker that acts as a warning to ships

carbon fibre very light and very strong building material

cargo goods carried by a ship

catamaran boat with two hulls

CIA US government agency set up to gather information about potential enemies

crankshaft part of an engine that is joined to the pistons; it turns the up-and-down motion of the pistons into a circular motion

coast where the sea meets the land

cockpit small space in a racing boat where the crew sit

crew group of people who work on a boat or ship

cylinder tube-shaped part of an engine where fuel is burned

drag (also called water resistance) force that pushes against a boat and slows it down as it moves through the water

dry dock special harbour where ships can be kept out of water

equator imaginary line around the middle of the Earth, halfway between the North and South Poles

friction force that acts when two things rub together

gondola long, narrow, flat-bottomed boat used on canals; it is moved along by pushing on a long pole

hammock piece of cloth that hangs above the floor of a boat, used as a bed

hull main body of a ship that sits in the water

infrared type of light that cannot be seen by the human eye

liner big ship that carries passengers all over the world

maiden voyage ship's first voyage or journey

manoeuvrable able to move and turn easily

mast upright pole that sails are attached to

monohull ship with a single hull

nuclear missile weapon with huge destructive power

piston part of an engine that slides in and out of a cylinder

propeller part of a ship's engine that spins under water and drives the ship along

prototype version that is built and tested before the real thing is made

radar (RAdio Detection And Ranging) way of detecting things when they are many miles away

reconnaissance finding out information about an enemy

rivet short metal pin that fixes sheets of metal together

sailor member of a ship's crew

satellite device that circles the Earth, sending and receiving signals

sonar (SOund and NAvigation Ranging) method of detecting where things are under water

stable firm and steady

stern back end of a boat or ship

submarine ship that can travel under water

vessel another word for a ship or boat

wake waves that spread out from the back of a ship when it is moving forward

welder person who joins pieces of metal by melting the edges

Raintree would like to thank the following for information used in the book:
Lloyd's Register – Fairplay Ltd
ITOPF Ltd

INDEX

Titles in the *Mean Machines* series include:

Hardback   1 844 43164 9

Hardback   1 844 43161 4

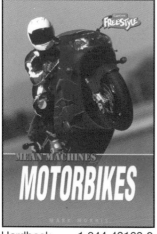

Hardback   1 844 43163 0

Hardback   1 844 43162 2

Find out about the other titles in this series on our website www.raintreepublishers.co.uk